Parable of the

WRITTEN AND ILLUSTRATED BY

Helen Caswell

ABINGDON PRESS
NASHVILLE

READ MATTHEW 13:33

Library of Congress Cataloging-in-Publication Data

Caswell, Helen Rayburn,
   Parable of the leaven/written and illustrated by Helen Caswell.
     p.   cm.—(Growing in faith library)
   Summary: A simple retelling of the parable which illustrates how the Kingdom of God enriches life.
   ISBN 0-687-30024-X (alk. paper)
    1. Leaven (Parable)—Juvenile literature. [1. Leaven (Parable) 2. Parables. 3. Bible stories—N.T.]
I. Title. II. Series: Caswell, Helen Rayburn. Growing in faith library.
BT378.L43C37   1992
226.8'09505—dc20
                                            92-15160
                                            AC

Printed in Hong Kong

At the store we buy a great big bag of flour
and a little tiny package of yeast,
which is also called "leaven."

At home in the kitchen we get ready to bake.

*I*n a big bowl we mix a spoonful of yeast with some warm milk, and then we put in lots and lots of flour.

*A*nd we let it rise.
The yeast makes it swell up
twice as big as when we started.

*T*hen we knead it and make it into loaves of bread.

And cinnamon rolls.

*A*nd all sorts of good things.

We wait until the yeast
makes them swell up twice as big again.

*T*hen we put them in the oven and bake them.

They come out warm and delicious
and light as a feather.
The yeast has worked like magic!

The Kingdom of God is like the yeast, Jesus said.
If we mixed the flour and milk without yeast,
It would turn out as hard as rocks.
The yeast makes it full of life and lightness,
and lots bigger than when it started!